C000301443

PICTURESQUE DYFI VALLEY

A
COLLECTION
OF
TWENTIETH-CENTURY
POSTCARD VIEWS

Gwyn Briwnant Jones

First Impression—2002

ISBN 1 84323 053 4

© Gwyn Briwnant Jones

Gwyn Briwnant Jones has asserted his right under
the Copyright, Designs and Patents Act, 1988,
to be identified as Author of this Work.

All rights reserved. No part of this book may be
reproduced, stored in a retrieval system, or transmitted
in any form or by any means, electronic, electrostatic,
magnetic tape, mechanical, photocopying, recording or
otherwise without permission in writing from the
publishers, Gomer Press, Llandysul, Ceredigion.

Printed in Wales at
Gomer Press, Llandysul, Ceredigion

Contents

Foreword

This fascinating visual record of the Dyfi Valley, in mid Wales, is based upon a collection of 171 twentieth-century postcards, illustrating 28 localities arranged in alphabetical order, with 60 featuring the town of Machynlleth and its immediate neighbourhood.

The compiler, Gwyn Briwnant Jones, a native of Machynlleth, is especially well-qualified in view of his detailed knowledge of the area and its history, and this is reflected in the informative captions which accompany the visual images. An acknowledged authority on railway history and a gifted artist specialising in re-creating 'railway' landscapes, he is fully aware of the important influence of railways on the development of local industries and settlements, on the growth of tourism and on creating an efficient postal system.

The combined effects of the attractiveness of the Dyfi Valley as a tourist area, and a remarkably reliable postal system led to the increasing popularity of the picture postcard, whose development as a *genre* is traced in the opening introductory section. Information is provided on the techniques adopted and on the various contributions to a flourishing postcard market of specialist postcard-publishing companies, such as Frith of Reigate and Valentine's of Dundee, printers from as far afield as Saxony as well as a number of local photographers, printers and publishers. The author traces the growth of the collection upon which this volume is based, which is confined to commercial postcards of local views, most of which were acquired by purchase or donation. Emphasis is justifiably placed on the importance of the postcard as a historical source recording local scenes, especially in an area such as the Dyfi Valley which had not attracted the attention of many artists and photographers in an earlier period.

Important historical associations include those linking Owain Glyndŵr with Machynlleth and Pennal; the legendary brigands, *Gwylliaid Cochion Mawddwy* with Mallwyd; the artist Richard Wilson with Penegoes, and the Londonderry family with Machynlleth. A number of the localities depicted have changed significantly since they were photographed and this is especially true of the scenes recording coastal shipping activities at Aberdyfi. Demolished buildings include the Grand Hotel, Borth; the older part of Plas Aberllefenni; and the Market Hall and later Town Hall in Machynlleth. Some buildings have been converted to other uses and these include the almshouses built by the Londonderry family in Machynlleth, which later became a private residence.

The quality of the reproduction of the period photographs is exceptionally high. The provision of relevant postal details and the personal messages which appeared on the cards indicate both the widespread distribution of the cards, again reflecting the increasing importance of tourism in this area, and also the essentially personal associations which were originally responsible for the purchase and transmission of the postcards. Featuring the landscapes, buildings, people, activities, costumes and vehicles, these cards will surely evoke reminiscences and interest, especially as they are accompanied by well-informed commentary. The volume will be treasured equally by local residents, visitors to the area, and those with personal associations with the Dyfi Valley. The extremely attractive presentation will further ensure a wide appeal, with readers appreciating a most proficient compiler's expertise in exploiting essentially ephemeral publications to portray various aspects of the history and life of a number of distinctive communities in mid Wales.

D. Huw Owen.

Introduction

Wales, land of rivers, mountains, lakes and vales – and with a coastline as varied as any. The grandeur of the north is well known, while the shy beauty of the former industrial valleys of the south seems to increase with each passing season.

Compared with these regions, relatively fewer people occupy the more remote central areas of the country. Here, the Severn and the Wye formed most of eastern mid Wales whilst, to the west, the majestic Mawddach and gentler Dyfi carved their way towards Cardigan Bay. The latter usually commands less attention than its more dramatic, northern neighbour although it has provided a backcloth for many notable events in our history and is the nearest we have to a natural border between north and south.

With the possible exception of the work of a few eighteenth- and nineteenth-century artists, the topography of the region was largely unrecorded until the advent of photography. Even then, the vision of the earliest photographers was restricted as they generally concentrated on people rather than places. It was not until the introduction of holidays for the working classes that photographers began producing 'popular' views, to be printed in their hundreds. They were thus the first to devote more concerted attention to the settlements and the natural beauty of the region.

What follows is a visual record of Machynlleth and the valley of the Dyfi, seen through their lenses; it constitutes a simple tribute to both their artistic vision and commercial enterprise.

For the purpose of this volume, the natural boundaries of the valley have been extended in a few instances to embrace some of the more important tributaries and adjacent areas – an action prompted partly by historical association and partly by the availability of cards.

The Development of the Picture Postcard

The picture postcard in its present form first appeared in January 1902, although its origins may be traced to the mid 1860s. The timely appearance of *Picturesque Dyfi Valley* serves to celebrate the centenary in mid Wales.

The concept of posting an open message on a plain card was officially introduced on 1 October 1869, in Austria. The idea was approved in Britain exactly a year later when court-size Postal Stationary Cards (approx. 4½ ins x 3½ ins) each bearing a pre-printed postage stamp, became available for ½d; the address occupied one face, the message was written on the reverse. By September 1894 the first British cards to be printed without a postage stamp were introduced. Illustrations – which commandeered most of the space previously reserved for the message – then began to appear; they proved to be extremely popular. From 1 November 1899, the Post Office accepted the larger size (approx. 5½ ins x 3½ ins) which had already been introduced on the continent; thereafter, this has become universally regarded as the standard postcard size. Finally, from January 1902, divided backs, providing space shared equally by message and address, were introduced.

The initial growth of the postcard industry co-incided with the increase in popular holidays and took full advantage of the efficiency of the railway-based postal service. Occasionally, cards are discovered today which demonstrate the dependability of the service as well as the frequency of collection and delivery. A card posted in the morning, with a message which declares, 'Will see you later this afternoon', bears silent testimony to the efficiency and reliability of the Post Office at that time – and to the confidence displayed by the sender.

Home photography was virtually non-existent at the turn of the century; only the well-to-do had time and money to indulge the hobby, and there was a ready market in almost every locality for commercially produced views of notable buildings or attractive scenery. The humble postcard thus became an early example of artefacts now referred to as 'collectable' – items spawned by man's ability to produce identical objects in their thousands, as a result of processes developed during the industrial revolution.

The period from 1902 to 1914 is generally regarded as the 'golden age' of postcard collecting, when most families of means sent and collected cards, the collections often being proudly displayed in dedicated albums. They were as important a component of Edwardian family life as the home video today. Great social changes occured, inevitably, as a result of the First World War; thereafter, interest waned and when postage was increased to 1d. by 1919, the numbers of cards produced were much reduced. Yet, the *genre* survived, through the years of depression and the Second World War, and during the last two decades of the twentieth century there was something of a renaissance, not only in the collecting but also in the sending of postcards.

Social historians today acknowledge that without the endeavours of the early postcard photographer – admittedly only in the business for his own gain – our knowledge of the appearance of towns and villages a century ago would be extremely scant. Frequently, the postcard photographer was the only person to record everyday scenes, scenes which may since have changed out of all recognition. As many of the earliest cards have been thoughtlessly discarded over the years, the survivors are treasured and nowadays change hands, in specialist postcard fairs, at prices which would not only astonish but completely mystify the collector of a century ago.

The majority of the early cards were produced by a photogravure process, whereby a photograph was etched on to a copper plate for later reproduction by letterpress printers. The major cost lay with production of the plate but once this was achieved, a local printer could produce hundreds of cards very cheaply. Thus, although a number of large companies flourished in the postcard business – famous names such as W. H. Smith, Frith of Reigate or Valentine of Dundee – a great number of smaller entrepreneurs were encouraged to exploit lucrative local markets. The Machynlleth area, for example, benefitted from the endeavours of several local people. E. Alfred Jones, newsagent and bookseller, published many views of the town over the years. A few were produced for him by one or other of the larger concerns, but most were printed in the town itself, many by R. Llewelyn Jones, also a printer and publisher. John Evans, of Albion House, Maengwyn Street, was another local printer who entered the profitable card market; he even named his house after his faithful printing press. One of the largest postcard companies in mid Wales, Park & Son of Newtown, produced a great many cards in the popular 'Park for People' series and mid Wales also featured prominently in the unusally named 'Wrench' series, which were printed in Saxony. Gwilym Williams, who dominated the retail market of cards of the Aberdyfi area, was another who published his own postcards, as did Evans & Son, Grocers of Penegoes and E. Evans of the Post Office, Dinas Mawddwy. Although many of their cards appear to have been printed on the continent they were proud to carry the imprint 'British Manufacture Throughout' whenever they could.

In time, pictures produced by photogravure were superseded by half-tone illustrations, a method which replaced the copper plate by a cheaper metal block. This could sometimes result in a coarser image; much depended on the quality of the screen used to produce the block. The best results of all were those produced directly from an original negative, in the form of a photographic print. Provided this had been exposed and developed carefully, prints of outstanding quality and definition could result. Yet, despite this superior quality, photographically produced cards were not numerous in the early days. Each had to be printed by hand – a much slower and more expensive process than producing a photogravure image. Consequently, photographic cards did not really gain popularity amongst manufacturers until costs were reduced by mechanising the printing process.

Another who served the Machynlleth area well was Donald Stuart George, born in Scotland in 1861. A competent and industrious photographer, he was initially apprenticed to Valentine's of Dundee where he received thorough training and gained valuable experience. Even when he ran his own business in Wales, he maintained a life-long working relationship with Valentine's. George met his wife-to-be whilst staying in the Barmouth area; they settled in Upper Corris when, in typical Welsh fashion, he rapidly became known as *George Top Corris*. During this period he established a successful photographic business at his home in Bryn Idris – where he had a studio and processing facilities – being the first house in Upper Corris to boast a piped, cold water supply. Periodically, he undertook work for the Egyptian Government and spent much time away from his Corris base. In addition to portraiture and other commissioned work, George generated a great many postcard views for the burgeoning tourist trade; around twenty-four examples grace these pages. Not only was the immediate locality recorded but a broader area extending from Barmouth and Dolgellau in the north to Aberystwyth in the south. George was also adept at capitalising on natural disasters within the district; landslides seem to have been particularly profitable for him! (see pages 35 & 106). Virtually all George's cards are characterized by extremely neat titles which were hand-drawn – in reverse – on each glass-plate negative. He used a variety of imprints over the years but, in the interests of uniformity, he is referred to here as D. S. George & Son.

It will be noticed that several of the images which follow have been trimmed in order to maximise the use of page area or emphasise certain aspects of the various compositions. Whilst this has the advantage of avoiding constant repetition of the universal postcard format, it also means, regrettably, that some of the original titles have had to be sacrificed.

The Development of the Collection

This collection is confined to commercial examples of local views which appeared in postcard form. It originated with a simple ambition to trace a few examples of the cards which once adorned the postcard carousels outside W. H. Smith in Maengwyn Street or E. Alfred Jones, Corner Shop, during the 1940s. From the half-dozen sepia cards initially acquired their numbers increased twenty-fold. As the collection has expanded, so also has the realisation that the format of the humble 5ins x 3ins postcard provides the single, most comprehensive archive of the growth of many towns and villages during the twentieth century; Machynlleth is no exception.

Most of the cards were purchased individually, or donated by friends. Inevitably, the interests and aims of individual collectors vary; some disregard cards which have been used postally or are badly worn whilst others will not purchase cards unless they have been used. A personal view is that the appeal of each card rests primarily with the pictorial quality of the image but it is a bonus if the card was also used postally as the message, recipient's address, the stamp itself or the franking, can all increase the item's general appeal. Attempting to define the year when a photograph was taken can be hazardous, but dates are offered whenever possible. Where none is available, but a card has been used postally, posting details are included but these provide only a rough guide to the date of the original photograph; in some instances a card may be used a decade or more after it was first printed. Where no date is available an estimated year is offered; if readers can suggest (and substantiate) a more accurate date, they are most welcome to contact the author or publisher, when any assistance will be acknowledged.

A conscious effort has been made to avoid repetition of views published previously but a certain degree of duplication is inevitable. It is hoped, however, that when this is unavoidable, the cards chosen will convey the atmosphere of different periods during the century.

Gaps are inevitable in a collection of this nature; they arise not from any disregard of settlements like Abercegir, or Ynyslas, for instance, but occur simply because no views of these districts have, as yet, been forthcoming. Accordingly, a few cards have been borrowed from the collections of The National Library of Wales, Aberystwyth, or from other friends; each has been acknowledged appropriately. Meanwhile, the fact that no one knows with certainty how many cards exist contributes to the fascination of the hobby. Who knows what may turn up next?

Plain Cards

Simple, plain, business postcards preceded the illustrated variety and are thus presented before the main collection. Although measuring just 4¾ins x 3ins, they typify the main means of communication used by Victorian businesses, long before the days of telephone, fax and e-mail. They demonstrate well the efficiency of the conventional Victorian postal system.

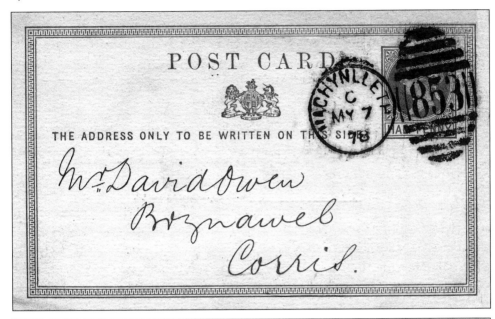

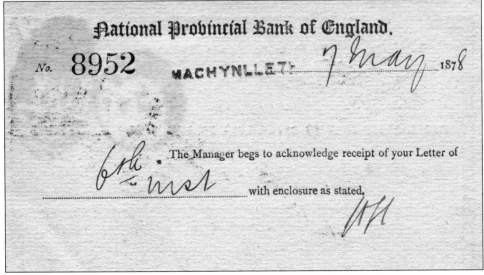

The message on this bank card, as might be anticipated, is brief and direct.

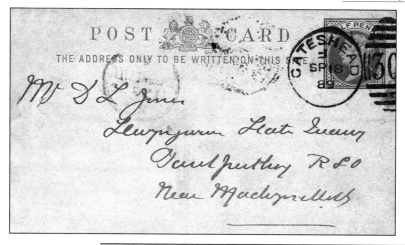

The enquiry to Llwyngwern quarry from Gateshead is equally succinct but additionally, reveals the high level of expectancy of the sender. The message reads,

> Dear Sir,
> Have you got the following slabs in stock and what is the price
>   1 slab 5.10 x 4.7 x 1¾
>   2 ”   5.10 x 3.1 x 1½   All good & sound
>   2 ”   4.1 x 3.1 x 1¼
>   1 ”   5.0 x 3.6 x 1½
> If you have not got the slab 5.10 x 4.7 we could manage with it in two say 4.7 x 2.11 & 4.7 x 3.0½ but all must be perfectly sound and free from cracks let us know by Friday morning. Signed.

Punctuation may have been minimal but all relevant information is included and the expectation of the enquirer is reflected in the final part of the message . . . 'let us know by Friday'. The card was dated and posted on 18th September 1889 . . . which was a Wednesday. A similar arrangement could hardly be entertained with the same confidence today.

Picture Postcards

ABERANGELL

During the 1860s, slate products from the quarries in the Hendre Ddu region were conveyed by narrow-gauge tramway to meet the Cambrian Railways Dinas Mawddwy branch line at a location about 4 miles north of Cemmes Road, where Afon Angell, a tributary, joined the Dyfi.

The development and expansion of Aberangell and the slate industry were therefore closely related. Most of the dwellings were erected on the wooded slopes west of the railway and river, creating an attractive, almost alpine, ambience which might be expected to have generated many picturesque views; but this is the only card seen to date.

This card was sent by a mother in Machynlleth to her daughter, staying with friends in Shepherd's Bush, in July 1906. It still carries the message:
Gobeithio dy fod yn mwynhau dy hun a bod y tywydd yn ffafriol.
[Hope you are enjoying yourself and that the weather is favourable].
(Park, Newtown, Mid Wales; c.1905.)

ABERDYFI

The two main reasons for the development of Aberdyfi were the ancient and long-established ferry across the estuary, which avoided a lengthy inland detour for north-south travellers, and the river itself, with the coves and bays of the northern shoreline offering sheltered anchorages for sea-going vessels. Before the coming of the railway during the mid 1860s, wooden vessels were constructed on the site of Penhelig Terrace and the railway halt. The new transport however, did not immediately destroy Aberdyfi as a commercial port, for the Cambrian Company developed and improved facilities in 1886, even promoting an ill-fated attempt, three years later, to establish a packet service to Waterford. Local minerals comprised the main export, the principal example being slate from the quarries at Aberllefenni, Bryneglwys and Corris. Shipments of potatoes and livestock from Ireland, timber from the Baltic, or commodities such as cement or grain from elsewhere in the UK, arrived regularly until the mid 1920s, yet the wharves and jetty were never as busy as in the larger Welsh docks.

This fine example of an early picture postcard is from the period when only a narrow vertical space (here omitted) was provided for a message; it was printed in Saxony. The schooner was the *Sarah Davies.* 1902
(The Wrench Series.)

Another early card, also printed in Saxony, posted from Aberystwyth to Leicester, 5 August 1903.

Three 'old salts' reflect on the past; two young lads dream of the future. Posted from Aberdovey (sic), 10 September 1904; no imprint.

Over the years, the commercial use of Aberdyfi harbour diminished and virtually ceased during the 1930s but the onset of the Second World War brought renewed activity to the river, albeit now related to military training and experiment. The coaster *Camroux III* was a regular visitor at this time, and there were others which came and went unrecorded. Since that period, the river at Aberdyfi has been dominated, increasingly, by small pleasure boats.

Transhipment at Aberdyfi around the turn of the century. In addition to the coaster alongside the jetty, the masts of two sailing vessels (one 2-masted, the other 3-masted) are just visible beyond the wagons, as also is a small rail-mounted steam crane which is assisting with the cargo. The crane was responsible for shunting the wagons around the wharf and jetty areas, which were prohibited to locomotives. Regrettably, it is not possible to make out the name of the small coaster. Card posted to Ulverston, 19 August 1905.

(The Wrench Series.)

Further evidence of activity at the wharves. This card was posted on 23 December, 1908:
Dear Cousin, Thank you very much for your letter and for the very nice memorial card . . .
(The Wrench Series.)

ABERDOVEY FROM THE ISLAND.

A card published by Gwilym Williams, Aberdovey (proclaiming *British Manufacture Throughout*) featured one of the smaller ferry vessels used latterly. Unhappily, the prominent white sail obscures what was possibly the largest of three sailing vessels alongside the jetty. *(Unused card c.1912.)*

Fronhaulog, Aberdovey

63023

Another Gwilym Williams card, also unused, c.1912.

This third card by the same publisher, whilst ostensibly portraying the elegant row of villas, also reveals maritime activity and a sizeable cargo of lumber being sorted by a steam crane amidst the sand dunes. Card posted on 5 May, 1918, to an address in Ebbw Vale:

I sent 2 silk blouses by post on Monday from here. I do hope you had them safe . . .

Signor Marconi used various parts of the coast of Wales for his early experiments with radio signals over water; his yacht the *Electra* was at Aberdyfi during August 1921 but, although this card was used postally, the stamp, with relevant franking details, was removed years ago by an over-zealous collector.

We have some very nice rooms and good food. It means a real rest for me and you cant (sic) imagine what a treat it is to me to have no preparing to do.

(Card was published for Gwilym Williams by the Photochrom Company Ltd., London & Tunbridge Wells.)

Gwilym Williams again . . . and proud of British Manufacture, but the original photograph carries the imprint of J. Valentine, of Dundee. The photographer made the most of a bevy of lissome ladies as they approached his camera, which rather leads one to suspect it might all have been pre-arranged! The card was posted on 23 July 1921:

> *The sea is very rough today. It is much cooler and we have had some welcome showers of rain . . .*

This half-tone sepia postcard, produced by J. Valentine of Dundee, featured Cliffside and Gray Jones' garage, alongside the lifeboat station, c.1928.

The first of two photographic cards in this section by D. S. George & Son suggests that although there is no activity on the river, the wharf continues to show signs of trade and a good eye-glass reveals a steam locomotive shunting between the warehouses and Glandovey Terrace (where it was allowed to operate). The card was sent to Liverpool on 15 October, 1931:

Such lovely weather we are having—I hope you are.

Bwlch Farm rests on the saddle between Abertafol and Cwm Maethlon, on the 'panoramic' route from Aberdyfi to the Bearded Lake. This was a popular walk for many visitors to the area during the first half of the last century. Bwlch proved a convenient resting place, where home-made teas were served in the lean-to alongside the barn, or outside, weather permitting. If walkers—who were always called 'visitors' during this period—chose to turn north immediately behind the house, they could wend their way down past Tyddyn-y-briddell to Cwm Maethlon; if they turned south, they enjoyed a delightful downhill walk past Braich-y-celyn, to Abertafol, before facing the choice of completing their journey to Aberdyfi by Crosville bus, train from the Halt, or continuing on foot.

(Unused card by Lilywhite Ltd. c.1925.)

Donald George again took to the high ground above Aberdyfi c.1930 when he photographed Penhelig. Until the construction of two tunnels for the railway caused spoil to be dumped on the foreshore, there was a sheltered cove here, used for shipbuilding. Initially, only one tunnel was intended, to the left of this composition; the rails were to emerge and curve right, across the estuary on what would have been a very fine bridge. Not only would this have incorporated a double line of rail but also a road on a lower level.

The scheme was defeated and the second tunnel opened, to give access along the north shore of the river, to Dyfi Junction. Later, a local builder took advantage of this elevated site and constructed Penhelig Terrace, and in 1933, the Great Western Railway opened Penhelig Halt, on the mound between the two tunnels.

Further details of this episode feature in *Railway Through Talerddig* (G. Briwnant Jones, Gomer Press, 1990 and 1992).

Aberdyfi from the Coast Guard Station, c. 1915.

(Unused card from the Wyndham Series.)

Penhelig, Aberdyfi, c. 1920.

(Unused card from the Wyndham Series.)

Cliffside, Aberdyfi, photographed possibly during the 1930s but the card was used postally in September, 1960.

I think its about time I sent you another P.C. the little dot is just over our front door . . .

(Valentine & Sons, Ltd.)

ABERHOSAN

Aberhosan nestles in one of the most picturesque regions of western Montgomeryshire, midst the lower (north-eastern) slopes of Pumlumon— an area which has been largely overlooked by photographers and artists.

Glyn Madian. This card was posted in Machynlleth on 22 September, 1905, to a Miss B. Ashton, in Newtown:

Hope to see you tomorrow starting from Machynlleth by the 2 o'clock train . . .

(Park, Newtown, Mid Wales.)

General view, looking north, showing the Post Office, Penygraig and the school. The card was posted in Aberhosan in 1935 but, judging by the appearance of the early motor car on the hill, the date of the original photograph might well precede the First World War.

(No imprint.)

General view of Aberhosan, looking west c.1965. Unused card.

(No imprint, but most likely Fitzwilliams, Seven Kings, Ilford.)

The Independent Chapel, photographed c.1965. Card used postally in 1968.

(Fitzwilliams, Seven Kings, Ilford.)

ABERLLEFENNI

The village of Aberllefenni takes its name from the nearby Plas, a site which has been occupied since at least the sixteenth century when, according to local historian, the late J. Arthur Williams, the house was known as Plas Llwyfeni (*llwyfen* – elm tree). Here, the word 'aber' signifies the confluence of the small brook from the Hengae Valley (upper illustration, overleaf) and the infant Afon Dulas.

Undoubtedly, the present village of Aberllefenni owes its existence to the quarrying industry. Slates for roofing and slate-slabs used in building, as laboratory working surfaces, electrical switchboard bases and beds for billiard tables, have been quarried in this region of south Meirioneth for decades and the Aberllefenni quarry—which produces slabs of the highest quality—is currently the only working quarry remaining in the district. Hopefully, a combination of safe and modern methods of production, a strong commercial demand and an abundant supply of finest quality rock will ensure the quarry's continued success.

Aberllefeni. No. 1.

This view by Park, of Newtown, seemingly No. 1 of a series, features the row of quarry-workers' cottages at Pensarn, opposite the main quarry sheds, workshops and waste tips. The card is unused and appears to date from c.1905. Nothing is known of card No. 2 nor the possibility of any subsequent views.

This charming composition almost constitutes an ariel view of the parts of the village featured in the previous illustration. The card was posted on 9 August, 1924, but the original photograph must pre-date this period by fully 10 years or more. Sent to an address in Great Yarmouth, the brief message, which is unsigned, declares:

This house is just above here and the end house is where we do our shopping.

(Valentine's Series.)

Plas Aberllefenni has a long history; it was the home of Sir John Lloyd, a sergeant-at-law in 1624, and was regularly visited during the eighteenth century by the Campbells of Stackpole Court, Pembrokeshire. The wing on the left of the photograph survives, but the older part of the house was demolished, partly in 1922 and finally, in 1975.

(Photograph c.1910 D. S. George & Son.)

ARTISTS' VALLEY

Artists' Valley or Cwm Einion, to use the Welsh name, lies some six miles south of Machynlleth; it was carved by Afon Einion *en route* from the heights of Moel-y-llyn and Pencreigiau'r Llan to join the Dyfi at Glandyfi. The picturesque waterfall and mill – visible from the main A487 road at Furnace – rather suprisingly, has not featured in any card to come the compiler's way.

(Unused Valentine's Card, courtesy of The National Library of Wales.)

This view was taken approximately half-way along the valley, looking east towards Dolgoch.
(D. S. George & Son, Real Photograph c.1920.)

BORTH

As it does not actually lie alongside the river, Borth is not often considered part of the Dyfi valley. Yet it lies on a storm beach, adjacent to the sand dunes, mud flats and salt marshes of the estuary and within the hills carved during the ice age. At low tide, stumps of alder, birch and scots pine are visible on the beach between Borth and Ynyslas Turn; sufficient evidence that the coastline, at the end of the ice age, lay around six miles further west, and fodder for the fable of Cantre'r Gwaelod and the Bells of Aberdyfi.

When the railway was introduced to the area, the promoters entertained great ambitions regarding both Borth and Ynyslas and Thomas Savin, the adventurous entrepreneur and railway contractor from Oswestry, purchased most of the land on either side of the railway. Early buildings constructed at Ynyslas, however, were not successful, due to the unstable nature of the ground and the majority had to be demolished. One row of houses was actually dismantled and re-erected at Machynlleth. Borth, in contrast, offered firmer, though not ideal, foundations and Savin

This view of the Station Terrace, Borth, shows part of the main entrance of the Grand Hotel (on the left) and the fine row of houses Savin built on the opposite side of the road. By the time of this card (c.1912) the buildings were beginning to show the ravages of 30–40 years since construction; the stucco, particularly, appears in need of attention. The Post Office (where this card was franked 'Borth S.O.' in 1922) was located mid-way between the refurbished, white property and the station, conveniently close at hand—further evidence of Savin's planning.

(Cambrian News (Aberystwyth) Ltd.)

constructed his Grand (originally Cambrian) Hotel there; it was intended
that other hotels would be dotted strategically around Cardigan Bay. The
Grand, alas, has long disappeared but a walled garden at Ynyslas survives.
This was intended to supply fresh produce for the hotels and for export by
train to the midlands. Savin also established the Castle Hotel at
Aberystwyth, by enlarging a house designed originally by John Nash.
Following Savin's financial difficulties in 1866, this was placed on the
market but remained unsold until 1872 when it was purchased – for a
fraction of its original cost – by the nascent University of Wales.
Regrettably, Savin's schemes proved over-ambitious.

PANT-Y-FEDWEN, BORTH.   W. 1264.

The Grand survived as an hotel until the outbreak of the Second World War, when it was
requisitioned and used by a college evacuated from London. In 1946, it was purchased by
the Pantyfedwen Trust, and re-named accordingly; it served Urdd Gobaith Cymru until
mounting costs caused its sale, c.1966.

(Published by Valentine & Sons, Dundee, c.1947.)

BWLCH-Y-GROES

No picture postcard of Graiglyn Dyfi, the small lake nestling directly beneath the summit of Aran Fawddwy (2971 ft) and the source of the river, has yet been discovered, therefore it is necessary to regard Bwlch-y-groes as the head of the Dyfi Valley in this context.

The Pass of Bwlch-y-groes is traversed by the steep and narrow minor road from Dinas Mawddwy to Llanuwchlyn, near Bala, a route which was long regarded as a severe testing ground by the manufacturers of early motor cars and cycles.

Arran Mawddy from Bwlch-y-Groes   Valentines Series

This distant view of Aran Fawddwy fails to convey any impression of its height, nor of the small lake at its foot, which is the source of the river Dyfi. Nonetheless, it affords a glimpse of the infant river's route as it cascades from its mountain source.

This delicately tinted photogravure card was also issued in a sepia version.

(Unused card from the Valentine Series, courtesy National Library of Wales, Aberystwyth.)

An unused example of Valentine's Carbo Colour Series, depicting an early motor-cycle and side-car breasting the summit of the pass, c. 1925.

This card, published by E. F. Russell of Barmouth, and posted from Machynlleth to Croydon in 1947, reveals more clearly the condition of the road surface during the 1920s and '30s as another motor-cycle combination negotiated the pass.

Dear Bert, This is where one's cycle really does become a 'push-bike', both up and down. This hill rises 1156 ft. within a mile with 200 yards of 1 in 4½ . . .

Enlarged section of the photogravure card
opposite, on page 27.

A mid-1960s 'Real Photo' card by Valentine & Son, posted from Llandrindod Wells to
Weston-super-Mare in 1966.

The same section as that featured in the
enlargement of the photogravure card (top
of this page) demonstrating the detail
superiority of the photographic card
opposite, on page 27.

This and the following card present two versions of the same original photograph and illustrate the broad differences between the photogravure process and a photographic print. This photogravure version provides a sound general impression with basically good contrast, but lacks fine detail. This particular card was used postally when it was sent from Tŷ Uchaf, Llan-y-mawddwy to Bala, on 19 May 1910. Instead of travelling the shorter 14m. route directly over the pass, it probably went via Machynlleth, Shrewsbury and Chester, a journey of approximately 155m.

> *Your parcel is to hand safe this morning. Thanks very much for your kindness, it was above our expectation . . .*   *(Valentine's Series.)*

The photographic card could have been marketed at any time during the 1930s, '40s or '50s. Although seemingly much darker in places than the photogravure version, it survives closer scrutiny under a searching magnifying glass and reveals greater detail, as is apparent in the same small section which has been enlarged from each card. It was not used postally, but is annotated on the reverse.

> *This is 6m. from Dinas Mawddwy and we're working over the other side about a mile or more . . .*   *(No imprint.)*

CEMAES AND CEMMES ROAD

When the railways wished to create a station where no settlement existed, they resorted to adopting the name of the nearest town or village and adding the word 'Road' to it. Experienced travellers soon realised that any station name ending in 'Road' was always a good distance from the place it purported to serve. Cemmes Road, spelt thus, presents a typical example; adapted in this instance from Cemmaes, Cemaes or Cemais—all versions of spelling the name of the village some mile and a half from the station. Similar examples in Wales are Pontypool Road, a mile or more from the centre of Pontypool and Clarbeston Road, in Pembrokeshire, some two miles from Clarbeston.

During construction of the Newtown & Machynlleth Railway, in the 1860s, the contractor, David Davies of Llandinam, initially referred to this location as Glantwymyn, a name which has enjoyed greater favour locally since the station closed.

Regrettably, no picture cards of Cemaes have yet come to hand.

As the hamlet grew around the station, it is virtually inevitable that the railway features prominently in cards of Cemmes Road. This particular example, by Park of Newtown, was over-printed by John Evans of Albion House, Machynlleth, as a Christmas card for his own use.

This was the view from the southern end of the 'up' platform, looking down the valley towards Machynlleth c.1925. The card, which has no imprint, was only partly written and although it carries an unused George V one penny stamp, it was never sent.

The Dyfi Valley from Abergwydol, looking west towards Llanwrin and Machynlleth, in the distance. The card was used as recently as 1997.

Many thanks for the lovely evening last week . . .

(Published by Evans & Son, Grocers, etc., Penegoes. Mont. c. 1920.)

Cemmes Valley with Mawddwy Railway

The Dyfi Valley near Cemmes Road, looking east and featuring the former Mawddwy Railway which closed finally in 1951.

(Unused card, c. 1930, courtesy of the National Library of Wales, Aberystwyth.)

Cemmes Road G.W.R. Station Yard and Mawddwy Branch Railway.

An interesting view of Cemmes Road, looking down the valley towards Machynlleth which, in addition to the main line station on the left, also affords a brief glimpse of the Mawddwy Railway platform on the right.

(Unused card, c. 1930, courtesy of the National Library of Wales, Aberystwyth.)

COMMINS COCH

It seems unlikely that Commins Coch ever achieved greater prominence than during consruction of the railway.

Once the engineers had decided that the best route from the Vale of the Severn to the shores of Cardigan Bay lay over Talerddig, Commins Coch found itself strategically placed midst important construction sites, as cuttings were excavated and bridges and embankments were built.

For a short period during 1862, the rails terminated here and the redoubtable David Davies even ran a Temperance Excursion for the good people of Oswestry, Newtown and Llanidloes to examine progress on the line although, at that time, there was no platform of any description at Commins Coch! Passenger facilities were non-existent and travellers were fore-warned that no refreshments would be available, but that did not stop a local entrepreneur from offering cups of tea for 1d. and buns for ½d.

COMMINS COCH. LOWER VILLAGE, No. 1.

The 'Park for People' series photographer visited Commins Coch c.1910; did he take further photographs, as the title suggests? This card, showing the railway on the embankment above the arch, was posted to Gelli, in the Rhondda, and carries a pencilled message:

Dear Tab, Just a PC to know that I am enjoying myself grand I am in this place today . . .

CORRIS

The two main veins of slate which run parallel in a south-westerly direction from near Minllyn, Dinas Mawddwy, to Bryneglwys just south of Abergynolwyn, were also worked at Hendre Ddu (Aberangell), Aberllefenni and Corris, where they were fairly near the surface and comparatively accessible. The village of Corris grew around several quarries in the immediate area.

During the greatest period of growth (c.1850–c.1900) Corris resembled a boom-town as homes, chapels, churches, shops and taverns were constructed; the population expanded and social activities thrived as choirs and bands were established and flourished. It was undeniably a strong working-class society but evidence of careful, frugal living, with occasional traces of capitalism, became evident as the more judicious saved hard-earned cash to purchase shares in various commercial ventures, including north Wales (and Merseyside) sailing ships. Although this was obviously regarded as a somewhat risky business, it generally brought better returns than offered by the local banks at that time.

Nor was it an uncultured society; the cabins where the men spent their meal breaks were forums for debate and centres of erudition, inspiration and motivation; many rose to prominence from the ranks of workers who started life in the quarries, Alfred W. Hughes being a typical but by no means solitary example. Amongst those who lived in Corris during the early decades of the twentieth century, and enriched its intellectual fabric, was one Egerton Phillimore, then Literary Critic of *The Times* newspaper.

The narrow-gauge railway, initially opened for the transportation of slate products in 1859, facilitated movement along the valley and provided access to Machynlleth and beyond; later, it was responsible for introducing the new 'tourist' classes to the area. Visitors came in their thousands to sample the scenic delights of the Dulas valley itself; at Corris they transferred to road vehicles, to witness the more dramatic vistas of Talyllyn and Cader Idris.

Today, the village of Corris is but a pale reflection of its former self but although the character of place and population has changed, there remains pride in the past and some optimism for the future, reflected in the successful promotion of new tourist attractions, on the site of Braichgoch quarry, or along part of the route of the old Corris Railway.

The company which operated Braichgoch Quarry encountered financial difficulties during the first decade of the twentieth century and was forced to suspend operation in 1906, failing to re-open until 1919. This card was posted at Corris, to Llanarmon, near Mold, in September, 1906.

Dear Mrs Langford, You see I am at home [but] going back to dirty London next Monday . . .

('Park for People' Series, Newtown, Mid Wales; c. 1905.)

Benjamin Pearce, the Machynlleth photographer, is not thought to have produced many postcards but this example, a real photograph, is credited to him in the annotation on the reverse, dated 25 April, 1906:

Another view of Fronwen. These two 'new' photos are by Pierce (sic), the watchmaker etc., at Machynlleth . . .

A second view has yet to come to hand.

Professor A. W. Hughes, F.R.C.S., was born at Fronwen, roughly mid-way between Corris and Aberllefenni, in 1861. He started his working life alongside his father in Aberllefenni quarry, before leaving to study medicine in Edinburgh, London and Leipzig. On his return, he was appointed Professor of Anatomy at King's College, London. Later, he left to establish a Welsh Hospital in South Africa during the war in 1899, but he died, tragically, on return to this country in 1900.

FRONWEN, CORRIS.
BIRTHPLACE OF THE LATE, PROFESSOR A. W. HUGHES, F.R.CS.

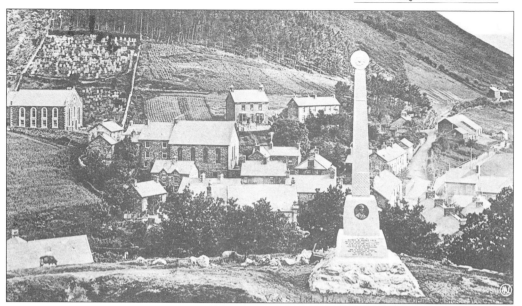

A view of the memorial to Professor Hughes, erected by public subscription, at Pen-y-braich
in 1905. Rehoboth Chapel, later destroyed by the storm in September 1922, is prominent on
the left of the picture. Posted in September, 1910, the card carried the pencilled message:

> *The country around here is simply lovely, wish you were here; I am going to Cader
> Idris today.*

(J. Valentine, Dundee.)

Corris, viewed from Fronfelen, looking towards a snow-decked Cader Idris (2928 ft). The
presence in the scene of the original Rehoboth helps to date the photograph as pre-1922,
possibly c.1920 or earlier. This particular card was written in the cafe at Dolgoch Falls and
posted from Towyn (sic) on 29 July, 1930.

> *Dear Daisy, We are having a fine time. The weather is lovely—just a little showery at
> times. We bathe lots and chase about. We are ever so brown already . . .*

(D. S. George & Son.)

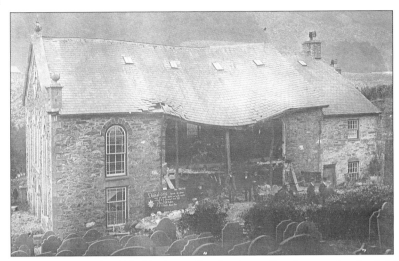

A severe cloud-burst on the hill-side immediately above Corris caused a landslide which tore through the cemetery, filled Rehoboth chapel to the height of the gallery with rocks, mud and other debris and continued downhill along a roadway which, only a short time previously, had been occupied by youngsters going to school. Had the slip been only yards further north, the school itself would have been threatened and, most likely, destroyed. But Corris was infinitely luckier than Aberfan, in 1966.

There are still those who remember the original Rehoboth as a handsome chapel. The circular window at the top of the gable, together with the roof lights, served a loft above the chapel, called Y Babell, used for Sunday School, Band of Hope and similar meetings.

(D. S. George & Son.)

Corris as seen from Braichgoch quarry c.1926, showing the position of the school (the twin-gabled building) in relation to the gap created by the demolished chapel. The light coloured building visible in the centre of the photograph, the new Rehoboth, was built alongside the road to Garneddwen and Aberllefenni.

(D. S. George & Son photograph, courtesy of the Corris Railway Society.)

The present Rehoboth, the Trinity Church and Braich-goch Farm feature prominently in the centre of this view of the vale of Aberllefenni, taken from Braichgoch Hotel gardens; the colourful umbrellas contribute to a holiday—almost Mediterranean—atmosphere. Unused card, c.1930.

(D. S. George & Son.)

Bridge Street, Corris, photographed c.1930. The black and white, half-timbered building is the Institute, provided by Sir Howell J. Williams, another of the illustrious sons of Corris who used his success in the wider world to benefit his native heath. He also provided most of the money to construct the new Rehoboth. Unused card.

(Maglona series.)

An interesting early photograph of Upper Corris, often referred to locally as 'Top Corris', taken around the turn of the nineteenth century. Amongst the features which contribute to its appeal are the traffic-free main road to Tal-y-llyn, the upper reaches of the horse-worked tramway from Maes-poeth, and the view of photographer D. S. George's home and studio, the prominent house in the right-hand, middle distance, identified by its large windows and skylight. This card was amongst those which appear to have been marketed jointly by Valentine's and George. It was not used postally until July 1920 but it obviously pre-dates that period.

4 Idris Terrace, Upper Corris RSO, I am sending you a few gooseberries, hope Amy will like them. The sweet ones have been taken by someone unknown to mother . . .

(*J. Valentine and D. S. George & Son.*)

An unused, almost mint example of another early card, possibly published in the district. The corrugated zinc-clad church in the foreground, formally termed Christ Church, was a satellite of Trinity Church, Corris, but was normally referred to, rather predictably, as '*eglwys sinc*'. It was built in 1886 and saw its last service around 1920. The church appears in good condition here and the card could be dated c.1905.   (*R. Morgan, Wales.*)

A particularly fine view of Glandwyryd Terrace, Upper Corris, perhaps around 1910. The combination of the light and the photographer's technique ensures that even the slates on the roofs could be counted if need be! Siop Tynyffridd, to the left, was run by a Miss Jones, around this time, who sold both general goods and clothes. The coal-cellar doors, at road level, are notable features of the terrace. The workings on the hillside are believed to be the Ty'n-y-ceunant quarry, which had ceased operation by 1875–8.

> *Do you remember this place? You see the chapel, a garden and then my home next to the garden—the end house ... A . C. Jones.*

                                                                                (D. S. George & Son.)

George certainly did his adopted locality proud. The quality of this image suggests the print was produced in the 1950s but the complete absence of any form of motorised transport, either on the farms, around Ty'n-y-berth school, or on the main road suggests an earlier date for the photograph itself. The telegraph poles alongside the road help to indicate a period during the late 1920s–early 1930s.

                                                                                (D. S. George & Son.)

This particular card was not used postally until 1970 but the original photograph dates from the early 1950s, before the school was re-located on the King George VI Coronation Playing Field.

(Courtesy The Francis Frith Collection, www.francisfrith.co.uk)

Largely through the efforts of local councillors (John Parsons, Bryn Edwin Stores and Mr Roberts, Abercorris Stores foremost amongst them) Corris acquired a new school building in 1955, when the Primary School was re-located on part of the King George VI Coronation Playing Field. Aberllefenni and Ty'n-y-berth schools were then closed. By the time of this photograph, other changes were apparent; most of the slate tips were beginning to mellow into the landscape and the reign of the D. S. George & Son photographic team had ceased with the death of Stuart George, the son, in 1953.

(Courtesy The Francis Frith Collection, www.francisfrith.co.uk)

CWM-LLINAU

Between Cemaes and Dinas Mawddwy the A470 trunk road cuts across the lower edge of the village of Cwm-llinau. Normally, it is hardly noticed by motorists on this busy north-south route other, possibly, than as a place where extra vigilance is required to negotiate the narrow bridge over Afon Llinau.

View, looking north, on the approach to the village. The road has been widened but the bridge is little altered.   *(Unused card, c.1910; no imprint; courtesy of Mrs G. Burton.)*

A composite card, with the earliest photograph dating certainly from the 1920s, possibly earlier. The popularity of this style spanned many years; this particular example was used postally in 1942.   *(A Raphael Tuck & Sons Ltd. card, courtesy of Mrs G. Burton.)*

Rural communities have to rely heavily on various forms of private transport. This group of interesting vehicles, from the coal-merchant's delivery lorry in the distance to the neat and well cared-for private cars in the foreground, rest on a minor road which joined the A470 at this point. The small, black Austin carried a Merionethshire (FF) registration plate, whilst the two-tone Hillman was first registered in Caernarvonshire (JC).

(An unused card, produced by Landscape View Publishers,
Market Harborough, courtesy of Mrs G. Burton.)

This slightly more recent view includes the Village Hall, as well as a post-war motor car in the middle distance (FEP 78).

(Unused real photograph card, by Photoway of Fleet Street, courtesy of Mrs G. Burton.)

CWM MAETHLON

Cwm Maethlon is the popular Welsh name for the quiet east-west valley formed by Afon Dyffryn Gwyn, north of Aberdyfi and frequently referred to as Happy Valley. It may be entered from the east by leaving the Machynlleth-Aberdyfi road at Cwrt, and following the narrow single-track road for approximately 1 mile to Pen-y-bwlch. Here the descent towards Tywyn sees the road passing through an increasingly fertile area, which gave it its name – '*maethlon*', literally translates as 'nourishing'. Nowadays, most traffic between Machynlleth and Tywyn travels by way of Aberdyfi leaving the narrower, picturesque route through Cwm Maethlon as a pleasant diversion for those who know of it.

View from Pen Bwlch, Happy Valley

This remarkably well preserved early colour card shows the view from the highest point on the road, looking towards Cwrt and Machynlleth.

(Published in Valentine's series, c.1905.)

It may be difficult to believe that Edwardian holiday-makers were so well dressed for lengthy country walks, but the evidence is here.

(Unused card, from the Wrench series, c.1903.)

A picturesque close-up of Afon Dyffryn Gwyn, Cwm Maethlon.

(Unused card © Judges Postcards Ltd, Hastings 01424 420909;
courtesy of The National Library of Wales, Aberystwyth.)

DERWENLAS

Derwenlas stands at the highest navigable point on the Dyfi, a factor of less significance these days than in the past, when the village served as the port for Machynlleth and surrounding district.

Before the coming of the railway, various products of the region (typically, slates and other minerals, bark, wool or leather) were loaded into river boats, which were adequate for the journey down-river to Aberdyfi, for transhipment to larger vessels if necessary. In return, lime for improving the land, and manufactured goods were imported; much material, in the form of rails, chairs and sleepers were shipped in through Derwenlas for construction of the railway, before the cutting at Talerddig was opened.

Regrettably, no photographs are thought to exist showing shipping on this part of the Dyfi, but the view on this card provides a general impression of the village c.1905. The group of small children (lower right corner) stands on the old road from Morben. The card was used postally in 1906:

Dear Mother, We have had a little rain today, but not much . . .

(No imprint.)

A later, photographic card, taken from a similar but elevated position. The card was written in Welsh: *Dyma fi wedi dod gartre yn saff . . . [Here I am, arrived home safely]*, and posted in Llanrwst, in 1934, to Trefor, Llanwnda. The original photograph could date from c.1928–32.   *(No imprint, save Guaranteed Real Photo and British Manufacture.)*

Llugwy Hall Hotel is located on the northern bank of the Dyfi, directly opposite Cei Ward, Derwenlas, scene of much maritime activity before the coming of the railway. During the early decades of the twentieth century, it was a private residence, occupied by the Anwyl family. This card was inscribed on the reverse 'With best wishes from Mr & Mrs Anwyl.'
(Park for People Series, c. 1910, courtesy of The National Library of Wales, Aberystwyth.)

DINAS MAWDDWY

The approach to Dinas Mawddwy from the south, along the narrow road which later became the A470. The card, c.1910 has no imprint but carries an indistinct date in 1933, when posted:

> It has been snowing here today. Everywhere looks so nice. Thank you for the lovely presents. They are so nice. Mam had the one with red on it and I the blue—she will write a long letter . . .

(Courtesy Mrs G. Burton.)

Dr John Davies, Rector of Mallwyd between 1614-1644, was responsible for erecting the pack-horse bridge at Minllyn, Dinas Mawddwy (nearest the camera) and also Pont-y-cleifion, Mallwyd, featured on p. 96. It is not easy to put a date to this card, but perhaps c.1920.

(D. S. George & Son.)

The slate tips of Minllyn Quarry form an impressive backcloth to this view of the Buckley Arms Hotel. Although the quarry ceased production during the early years of the first World War, many of the buildings, together with those of the erstwhile railway station, nearby, now serve as a tourist centre. *(Valentine's Real Photograph No. 97642, c.1920.)*

The negative number of this view of Dinas Mawddwy, looking up the valley of the Cerist towards Dolobran and Bwlch Oerddrws, suggests it dates from around the same period as the previous view. Although not particularly sharp, in terms of photographic definition, it is still clear enough to see that Plas Buckley, in the centre of the village, is minus its roof, lost in a disastrous fire c.1920. The card was posted in 1926.

(Valentine's Real Photograph No. 97646, c.1920.)

Maes-y-glasau Falls, Bwlchoerddrws, Dinas Mawddwy, c. 1955. Posted in Dolgellau on 27 July, 1960, but written in Llwyngwril; *We are at a camp very near the sea. On Monday and Tuesday it was lovely. We had a thunderstorm late last night and it is drizzling this morning.*

(A Valentine's postcard)

Dinas Mawddwy and Plas, seemingly in good order. View looking west, towards Cemaes.

(Unused card by Photochrom Co. Ltd., c. 1915.)

ESGAIRFOCHNANT

Few would expect an area as comparatively remote as Esgairfochnant to feature in a picture postcard book. The demand for cards of the area must have been decidedly limited, even during the Victorian and Edwardian days of optimism and discovery; the chances of survival of such cards must be minimal. Thus, this view of Egairfochnant Rocks represents one of the more surprising discoveries during compilation of this collection.

A 1949 Guide book to Machynlleth and district suggests that 'these rocks . . . are a delight to the few who take the trouble to visit them. They are a great joy to climbers and those who like nature in a wild mood.' Even today, with the availability of various forms of off-road vehicles, it is good to realise that parts of mid Wales remain the province of hill-walkers, climbers and hikers.

Esgairfochnant Rocks, Machynlleth.

An unused and undated card which, judging by the appearance of the hiker, might appear to precede the First World War. It reveals the intrepid nature of many of the pioneer postcard photographers. It would be fairly safe to assume that, even today, very few take the trouble to visit this area, only about six miles from Machynlleth, although the creation of a new recreation path, Glyndŵr's Way, may encourage change.

(No imprint.)

ESGAIRGEILIOG

J. Arthur Williams, in *Trem yn Ôl*, suggests that the village of Esgairgeiliog did not exist at the turn of the eighteenth century, although a woollen mill and some houses, known as Caerbont, were erected soon afterwards. The village was not fully established until the boom in slate production, mid-way through the nineteenth century, the three most succesful quarries in the vicinity being the ERA (also known as the Colarado), the Cambrian Wynne and Rhiwgwreiddyn.

Esgairgeiliog is also known as Ceinws, a name borrowed early in the village's existence from a nearby farm but at various times, it has also been referred to as Aberglesyrch and Pentref Caerbont.

The decline of the slate industry has, to a certain extent, been partly offset by the growth in afforestation – the vast Dyfi forest, very broadly, 'following' the slate-bearing rock, from Minllyn and Hendre Ddu in the east, through Aberllefenni, Esgairgeiliog and Corris, to Bryneglwys near Abergynolwyn in the west.

This general view of Esgairgeiliog, dating from the very early years of the last century, shows the bridge of the old road from Corris to Machynlleth crossing Aber Glesyrch. How this card was chosen to be sent from Beverley, in Yorkshire, to Sutton-on-hill in August 1905 must remain a mystery.

(Courtesy The Francis Frith Collection, www.francisfrith.co.uk)

FORGE

The hamlet of Forge is located approximately a mile from Machynlleth, where the mountain road to Llanidloes (via Dylife and Staylittle) and the minor road to Uwchygarreg, Ceniarth and Talbontdrain, bifurcate.

When the woollen industry and associated trades flourished in the Machynlleth area, before the coming of the railway, good use was made of the abundance of clear, running water in the district in order to run water wheels and mills. The hamlets of Forge and Felingerrig, lower down the river, were typical locations for such activities.

Later, the river was used to generate hydro-electric power for the town, at Dolgau, just down-river from Forge. As demand for electricity grew, a second power station was opened, again on the same river, near Felingerrig.

A view looking up the valley of the Dulas at Forge. Card posted from Machynlleth, 14 August, 1906:

Dear Mrs Robinson, We are having a nice time here . . .   *(No imprint.)*

GLANDYFI

Glandyfi was another point on the Dyfi notable for modest ship-building and coastal trade. It was called Garreg before the coming of the railway which, initially, threatened to isolate the area completely (see *Railway Through Talerddig*, G. Briwnant Jones, pp. 74–5). That scheme, however, was defeated and the railway later made amends by bringing many visitors who wished to sample the rural delights of nearby Llyfnant valley; Glandyfi was a popular starting point for the walk, particularly for those who were holidaying along the coast.

Glandyfi Railway Station.

The distinctive style of caption again identifies this card as one of the 'Park for People' series. Carrying a clear 'Eglwysfach' post mark, as well as a legible 'Glandyfi RSO' (Railway Sorting Office) mark, the card made its way on 31 December, 1905 to Llanarmon, near Mold.

> *Lle unig iawn sydd i weld ar y cerdyn . . . er . . . y city yn fywiog iawn, fel y gadawsoch hi. Cyfarfodydd da iawn yn ddiweddar. Blwyddyn Newydd dda i chwi. Baden Powell.*

> [A very lonely place to be seen on the card . . . but . . . the city is very lively, as you left it. Good meetings recently. Happy New Year to you. Baden Powell.]

(Park for People series, c. 1905.)

The locomotive with the Aberystwyth-bound train was one of six former Metropolitan Railway engines purchased by the Cambrian in November 1905; they ran initially with highly polished domes, as in the illustration, which helps to date this card c. 1906.

('Maglona' series; unused card, published by R. Llewellyn Jones, Papyrus, Machynlleth.)

Glandovey Castle.

. . . What a pity we are having so much rain . . . I hope you are still enjoying yourselves. This castle is quite close to us. We passed it last Thursday on our way to Llyfnant Valley—I have never seen such fine scenery anywhere.

(No imprint, but posted at Aberdyfi (Pant Eidal address) on 21 August, 1910.)

The beauty of Glandyfi is hardly reflected in this particular composition, yet it serves to remind us that the Great Western Railway thought sufficiently of the Llyfnant Valley to incorporate the name on a station name-board. This card was posted at Eglwysfach, 18 August, 1964, to Box Hill, Surrey.

(Landscape View Publishers, Market Harborough.)

Over the years, this view has been glimpsed briefly from train windows by literally thousands of passengers on the Cambrian line, west of Glandyfi. The photographer must have been standing on the railway formation as he photographed the little Einion river on its way to the Dyfi, beyond.   *(Unused real photograph card, c. 1930. D. J. Davies.)*

LLANBRYNMAIR

Llanbrynmair lies near the confluence of three important tributaries of the Dyfi, the Twymyn, which rises in the hills above Dylife, the Iaen, from near Talerddig and Afon Rhiw Saeson, which enters from the north. Amongst several prominent Welshmen who hail from Llanbrynmair may be noted The Revd. Samuel Roberts (SR), (1800-85), preacher, philanthropist, and originator of the penny post (he sold the idea to Rowland Hill); David Howell, (1816-90), Machynlleth solicitor who master-minded the coming of the railway to the valley of the Dyfi and Dr Iorwerth Peate, (1901-82), creator and first curator of the (then) Welsh Folk Museum at St. Fagans, Cardiff, now known as The Museum of Welsh Life.

When the railway was being constructed through the locality, the area was first referred to in the contractor's account books as 'Wynnstay' after the inn of that name. The railway still runs just north of the inn although nearby Llanbrynmair station, closed in 1965, survives as a private house.

Wynnstay Hotel, looking North, Llanbrynmair.

This is the only card of Llanbrynmair in the collection, but it presents a delightful record of road transport in the area during the late 1920s. The car appears to be a bull-nosed Morris, possible registration number EP 3222, whilst the delivery van also carries an old Montgomeryshire registration plate, EP 1(?)729. The bus (reg. no. TA8115) appears to be the most interesting of all; it was owned by the Corris Railway Company, which operated special market-day services from Machynlleth to Newtown each Tuesday, until the GWR acquired the company in 1930. By 1932, a daily through service was established by Western Transport, a subsidiary of the GWR; the Crosville Company took over in 1933.

(Unused card, no imprint, c.1927.)

LLWYNGWERN

Most of the houses in this area, together with the village school, were found in nearby Pantperthog, a few hundred yards to the south of the station which took its name from the local Plas and quarry. The Corris Railway chose this location as the gradient was more favourable than at Pantperthog; also the minor road which served the Plas, Pantperthog mill and Llwyngwern quarry, crossed the line on the level here. Somewhat ironically, therefore, Llwyngwern station was sandwiched between Pantperthog mill and Pantperthog village.

Corris Toy Train.

Although this particular card has been published previously, this copy is clearer than most; its title also shows how tourists regarded the narrow-gauge railway, which was certainly no toy but constructed for the utilitarian purpose of transporting thousands of tons of slates and slabs from the quarries to Derwenlas and Machynlleth. The siding to Llwyngwern quarry may be seen veering away to the right. During summer months, tourists patronised the trains in their thousands and the Corris Railway Society presently seeks to emulate this success by re-opening part of the route which was closed completely in 1948. Since 1975, the Llwyngwern quarry site has been transformed and is now established as the Centre for Alternative Technology, demonstrating new methods of energy conservation and environment protection. *(Unused sepia card, without imprint, c.1910.)*

LLYFNANT VALLEY

The Llyfnant Valley offers picturesque scenery of great charm, a fact that has been well appreciated by visitors to the district over a great many years. One indication of this popularity is that although within an afternoon's walk of Machynlleth, some, in the past, created the illusion that Llyfnant was near Aberystwyth!

In 1912, the area was threatened by the War Office, which proposed to create an artillery range near Glaspwll. Happily, common sense prevailed and as a result of strong local protests, the scheme was abandoned.

Thereafter, the Cambrian Railways promoted the valley as a tourist attraction with renewed vigour and special fares were available over a wide area of the coast. This, in turn, boosted the sale of post-cards; the number of different cards of Llyfnant and Glaspwll is quite remarkable—only a selection is presented here.

The first two examples date from the transitionary period when some cards still retained a space for a message below the illustration, as well as on the reverse. One wonders whether Mag was fretting about a boyfriend or her cat?

(Photogravure card from the Wrench Series, c.1903.)

Posted at Machynlleth on (Thursday) 13 August, 1903, the message continues on the reverse:

> We are at Aberystwyth since Monday, having high time, staying at the Waterloo Hotel. We are in this valley today, a party of 17 Aberdarians . . .

(Photogravure card, no imprint.)

Publicity at Aberystwyth was obviously worthwhile; this card was posted there on 22 August, 1904. Over the years Ty-mawr has been well-regarded for the quality of its hospitality.

(Photogravure card, no imprint.)

This example was also posted in Aberystwyth, but to an address in Machynlleth, on 25 August, 1904.   *(Photogravure card, 'Dainty' Series.)*

Sunday 1.0 p.m. 17-9-11, Dear Daughter, Dull morning with mist on sea but now, since half-an-hour, sun shining. Ain't I a queer man as good as saying that I would not go to Machynlleth at all & I've been twice, but the 2nd time was somewhat accidental. I was fortunate enough this time to see all that can be seen of Lord Tempest's home from the outside, & was taken through the stables. All the horses with the exception of 3 (which I saw) had that day gone to Scotland with His Lordship. This is the house where I got dinner yes on a table just where the dog stands. You shall hear more of this again, Much love Dad.

In addition to the above message, the sender just about found room for an address (in Chester) and a stamp!   *(No imprint, but posted in Aberystwyth on 17 September, 1911.)*

Dear Bell, We are going to this place to-morrow.
(WHS Kingsway Real Photo Series, posted at Machynlleth, 27 September, 1911.)

A further pair of fine cards by the reliable Mr George, c.1912.

(Unused, Real Photograph by D. S. George & Son.)

(Unused, Real Photograph by D. S. George & Son.)

MACHYNLLETH

Machynlleth has been the focal point of events in the Dyfi Valley since the middle ages. During that time, changes have been gradual and on a modest scale, for the town has grown comparatively little during the years. Nonetheless, its location near the lowest-bridging point on the river, and just two miles inland from the highest navigable point at Derwenlas, was sufficient to establish it as the main commercial centre for the region. Population has hovered around the 2000 mark for many years, for local industries were always on a modest scale. In the past, they were associated mainly with agriculture (weaving or tanning) or slate quarrying/lead mining: towards the end of the twentieth century, communications, forestry, light engineering, tourist or eco-friendly industries provided employment in the region.

The town's long and colourful history is most frequently recalled nowadays through its association with Owain Glyndŵr, in the fifteenth century, or with the Londonderry family in the nineteenth and twentieth centuries. There were other events and personalities, of course, but the shadow of the man who came close to unifying Wales in 1404, remains over the town. Similarly—although for different reasons—the influential family of the Plas, with extensive dock and mining interests in the Durham coal-field, lead-mining locally at Dylife and Van, and slate quarrying at Corris, also cast a spell over Machynlleth. There are still those who can recall, and perhaps wistfully regret, the passing of their influence. The Londonderry family, which was instrumental in providing central Wales with a railway system during the 1860s, also put the town on the social map of Great Britain when members of the royal family were entertained at the Plas in 1896 and 1911.

Most regrettably, many of the visual changes which took place in Machynlleth, particularly before the industrial revolution, have slipped by unrecorded. Even with the advent of photography, comparatively few graphic images exist to enlighten us. John Owen of Newtown photographed the excavation of Talerddig cutting in the 1860s, for example, but his topographic work including six widely advertised views of the construction and at least one photograph of the Grand Opening of the railway at Machynlleth in 1863, is largely lost. Fortunately, two photographs were converted into engravings for the *Illustrated News*; they survive only in this form. John Thomas, the itinerant Liverpool-based photographer was one of the first to record the area but his work, with that of other local photographers, was not generally issued in postcard form. When 'home photography' became available for the keen and affluent, from the turn of the century, those with cameras rarely displayed sufficient skill to produce successful prints which might be of general interest today. Several generations of photographers failed to appreciate that the commonplace, everyday scenes which surrounded them could fascinate future generations. We have all the more reason, therefore, to thank humble postcard photographers for many of the most interesting views taken during the first half of the twentieth century.

Almshouses

Dowager Marchioness of Londonderry Memorial, Machynlleth.

Londonderry generosity towards the town extended to construction of a hall, hospital, school and these alms houses, erected on the corner of Heol-y-Doll and Heol Penrallt, in 1868, by Mary Cornelia, Countess Vane at that time. The houses were let, free of rent, to townspeople deemed in need. The bust of Mary Cornelia, later the Marchioness of Londonderry, has since been re-erected in the grounds of the Plas and the almshouses have been converted into a private residence.   *(Card written but not posted, c.1910; no imprint.)*

Castlereagh Clock Tower

The Castlereagh Clock Tower was erected, by public subscription, to commemorate the 21st birthday of Charles Stewart Vane-Tempest, Viscount Castlereagh, on 16 July, 1873. This elegant example of the *genre* was completed and inaugurated by 31 August, 1875; it can be considered amongst the finest in Wales. Designed by Henry Kennedy of London and built by a local man, Edward Edwards, it reflects great credit both on them and the townspeople who responded to David Howell's appeal fund. The card was posted at Aberystwyth in July 1907. *(Valentine Series.)*

A more recent card, perhaps taken on a Sunday morning, showing little change in the clock or surrounding buildings. Only detail differences intrude: the black-and-white finger-post, road signs, traffic bollards, and two cigarette signs suspended above Ritchie Morgan's shop. Card posted from Machynlleth to Warrington on 6 September, 1967.

We are having coffee here this morning. Have been to places in Wales we did not know existed. Its lovely and sunny here now, after terrific high tides last night, lovely hotel. (© Judges Postcards Ltd, Hastings 01424 920919.)

County School

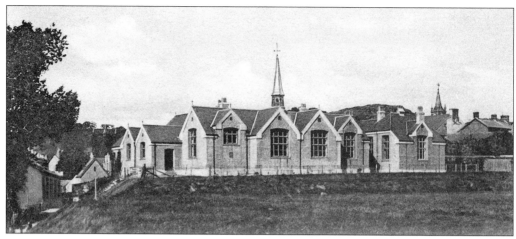

This fine view of what is nowadays regarded as the 'old' County School would appear to have been taken during the early years after completion, perhaps c.1900-5, although the card itself was not posted until November 1918, when a student of Warrington Training College wrote:

> *What do you think of the latest. Isn't it great. Voila l'ecole. It certainly looks at its best here—not really so nice.*
>
> *(Park, Newtown, Mid Wales.)*

Court or Mayor's Offices

These charming medieval houses are still occupied at the start of the twenty-first century but the era of their greatest prominence, undoubtedly, was from the late 1500s to the mid 1750s when they served as the most important offices in the region for the transaction of the manorial rights of Cyfeiliog, Arwystli, and for general administration of the town. A third gable was added after this photograph was taken. The title on the card, which was posted to West Norwood from Newcastle, Clun, Salop in 1927, is obviously an error.

(Published by J. Evans, Printer & Stationer, Machynlleth; Everton Series.)

Heol Maengwyn panorama (c.1910) features the half-timbered Court/Mayor's Offices on the left and, beyond, the newly erected Drill Hall (1909). The mode of dress of the ladies and the sight of cyclists, walkers and a hand-cart occupying the middle of the road, reflect the pace of life at that time. This photographic card was posted on 18 January, 1911, at Aberystwyth.

> *Dear Ma, Hope you are going on all serene . . .*

(Published by WHS, Kingsway Real Photo Series.)

Dyfi Bridge or Pont-ar-Ddyfi

Dyfi Bridge has changed little since this photograph was taken – it continues to cope with modern traffic demands

Posted to Rutland Gate, Knightsbridge, in April 1908, the sender worried, *Are you all keeping well; I have not heard from you lately? Send a postcard when you have time.*

(William Haddon, Publisher, Tipton, c. 1915.)

Recently, this view has gained added interest by the creation of a Millennium walk and cycle path at this point. By crossing the river on a new bridge on the site of the original, wooden Corris Railway bridge in the distance, this route avoids the congested and narrow road bridge. The card was used postally from Machynlleth to Shepherd's Bush in September, 1905.   *(No imprint.)*

Dyfi Bridge, seen from above the road to Corris, photographed c.1925-35. The card, posted in August 1952, carries the message:

> *This is a sample of the scenery around here & we have done quite 400 miles by coach touring around & seeing all the most interesting & historic places & thoroughly enjoying my holiday. Give my regards to our good treasurer (!) . . .*

(No imprint.)

Present-day volumes of traffic would make standing at this location on the bridge for the purpose of photography a hazardous business, but this view dates from the early 1960s. It was posted from Machynlleth to Hampshire in October, 1965.

> *Made it OK to here. Corris is wonderful. Mrs Davies had a fire on, the kettle boiled and bottles in the bed. The weather is too hot. Looks as if we did the right thing waiting till Oct.* *(© Judges Postcards Ltd, Hastings 01424 420919.)*

Pont Glanfechan

Evan Jones's answer to Llanfair PG c.1910. This card was over-printed and published in the Maglona series. *(E. Jones, Machynlleth.)*

Y Garth

A good example of the postcard photographer as recorder of rural aspects. The river appears to be smooth, even frozen, as the exposure was not instantaneous, c.1910.

(Unused card; no imprint.)

Y Graig

This view of Capel y Graig was taken from a corner of the old school-house yard, c.1910. The card was unused as a large ink blot was created accidentally when writing the address—an unknown hazard since the advent of the ballpoint pen.

(Park, Newtown, Mid Wales.)

Greetings

In addition to incorporating local views, this attractive composite card features the common seal, based upon that of Owain Glyndŵr, and adapted by Machynlleth Urban District Council when it was formed as a result of Local Government reform 1894–5. The designer can be forgiven for failing to interpret Owain's name correctly from a wax impression. The card was posted from Machynlleth to Aberystwyth in August 1906.

Here we are again, out for the day . . .   *(Spa Series.)*

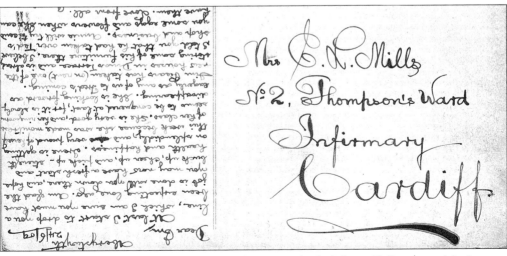

This example of fine penmanship featured on a card of Llyfnant Valley, posted in June 1909.

(No Imprint.)

General Views

This Town is of considerable antiquity, and probably in conjunction with a certain part of the adjoining parish of Pennal (situated both sides of the Dovey—extending from *Talgarth* near Pennal to *Garth* near Machynlleth) is the *site of the* Maglona of the itineraries,—an important Roman Station,—and on record since over 1800 years.

In the reign of the Emperor Honorius, the Captain of the *Numerus Solensium* was stationed here, under the *Dux Britanniarum*. Roman roads were passing through in four different direcrions, and Roman fortresses on *Penyrallt* and *Cefn Caer* were in action. Some Roman remains are still to be seen, and Roman coins at various times discovered at *Cefn* ,and on *Gallt-y-Gog*, near Machynlleth.—E.J.
(*Copyright.*)

When the new century was celebrated in 1900, this engraving served as a reminder of progress made during the previous hundred years. Regrettably it lacks sufficient accuracy to have much historic significance although Capel y Graig (1789) and the area of Graig Fach may be made out. The card, devoid of punctuation, was used postally from Machynlleth in August, 1905:

> *Dear Dad hope your feet are alright we are having a fine time but it is rather wet with love Ada*
> (*Maglona Series.*)

A more recent view, photographed c.1905, from much the same location on Penrallt as the previous illustration. The gradual development of the town may be traced superficially and it is possible to make out some older buildings alongside the field and allotments behind Maengwyn Street, as well as the large walled kitchen garden for the Plas, the County School, and the Clock Tower.
(*Valentine Series.*)

Virtually the same photographic location on Penrallt was chosen for this view, but this time looking south-east. Again, interesting buildings survive from an earlier era, behind Maengwyn Street; the foundry and Iorwerth Terrace (lower left) with the playground and the new Board School, suggest a date between 1905 and 1910.   (*Valentine's Series.*)

Town panorama from Yr Wylfa. The development of the County School, although partly obscured by trees and dense shadows created by the evening light, is already underway, and helps to date this general view around 1949.

(*'Maglona' Series, Jones, Corner Shop, Machynlleth.*)

Machynlleth

The most recent view, in this group, seen from just above the original viewpoint on Penrallt. The development of the town's car park, Cartref Dyfi and Graig Fach Flats all reflect the continuing process of development, but the Bro Ddyfi Leisure Centre has yet to emerge, c.1985.   *(© Judges Postcards Ltd, Hastings 01424 420919.)*

Heol-y-Doll

Machunlleth. Doll Street from Railway Station.   *"Park for People" Series.*

This was the view of Machynlleth seen by most railway travellers, c.1910. The building just beyond the former Police Station, on the left, was the old National School, built in 1829. The erroneous street-name – part English, part Welsh – should be either Heol-y-Doll or Toll Street.   *(Park, Newtown, Mid Wales.)*

This view of Heol-y-Doll affords a better view of the former National School, which was demolished and re-built in 1914, and the two rows of weavers' cottages beyond. The attractive front row is still occupied whilst the houses on the right form Railway Terrace. The young boy carting a loaded sack from the railway station, on a hand-cart, appears to be having difficulty with his load, c.1910.   *(Valentine's Series.)*

Railway Terrace, c. 1930. The garage was run at this time by a Mr Matthews, before H.G. Jones purchased the business in 1936.

(Maglona Series, Jones Machynlleth.)

Heol Maengwyn

No pavement existed when this early view was taken, c.1870. The old market hall was demolished shortly afterwards, to clear the site for the new town clock. This very early form of illustrated card allowed no space at all for any message as the reverse was devoted entirely to the address; little wonder, perhaps, that it was not posted.   *(No imprint.)*

Broad, tree-lined Maengwyn Street, before pavements were completed on both sides of the road; the Post Office was established at this time, indicating a period before the First World War, perhaps c. 1912. Some goods for D. T. Davies, the ironmonger, were unloaded from the Cambrian Railways horse-dray whilst, extreme right, a stray sheep or unidentified breed of dog made its way up the street. Card posted to Leebotwood, from Machynlleth, on 6 September, 1916. *(Maglona Series, published by E. Alfred Jones, Londonderry House, Machynlleth.)*

The wealth of detail in this photographic card has to be viewed through a good eye-glass to be fully appreciated. *Pratts* and *Shell* petrol is available from the roadside pumps, which survived on this site into the late 1950s. Two hackney cabs await hire, the furthest from the camera with a Montgomeryshire registration plate, EP 3148 and, across the road, WH Smith may be seen to have opened a branch. Motor-cycles for sale are parked on the right and a general increase in road traffic is apparent, c.1928.   *(Unused card; no imprint.)*

A post-war view with an Austin 'Devon' saloon, a pre-war Austin '8', a rear view of the Corris service bus outside the Post Office, a very nice Riley 1.5 outside S. L. Owen's shop (AEJ 300) and, by this time, a broken white line painted down the centre of the road. Photograph c.1956.   *(A real photograph card by Harvey Barton & Son, Bristol.)*

Only three pedestrians, and an equal number of cars, are visible in this 9.30 a.m. view of the Wynnstay Hotel and town clock.   *(Unused card published by Valentine's of Dundee c. 1958.)*

Although this may be considered a 'modern' scene, many of the cars featured in it will already have gone to the scrap-yard. The town itself, however, with its new civic colour scheme, looks as attractive as ever, c.1980-5.

(© Judges Postcards Ltd, Hastings 01424 420919.)

The first of two views, from much the same elevated position, but taken some forty years apart. A poster displayed outside E. Alfred Jones' corner shop reads 'More Planes for Britain', perhaps suggesting a date during the First World War, around 1916.

(Published in the Maglona Series by E. Alfred Jones, Londonderry House, V&S Ltd.)

After the Second World War: Alfred Jones's name survives above the corner shop, and the display cabinets are still full of postcards; Melias occupies the premises next door and Gwyn Evans, the Off Licence, takes advantage of the summer season to sell his own brand of ice-cream. Across the road, W.H. Smith still operate as newsagents and booksellers, whilst the Red Lion, Glasgow House, S. L. Owen, Jane's Gown Shop and Hugh Davies Drug Store are all prominent. Dr Dan Davies's MG *Magnette* is parked outside his surgery and other cars add to the increasing volume of traffic. Two of the registration numbers which are legible are 747 FMA (Rover 90, outside the Wynnstay) and Post Office van, BGH 382 about to turn into the Post Office. Two GPO telephone vans, with ladders on their roofs, are further up the street but not identifiable. Unused card, c.1956.　　　*(Valentine's 'Real Photo'.)*

This is the final view of Maengwyn in this section. In the centre of the composition, a young postman, probably having collected a load of mail from the railway station and on his way to the new Post Office, could not resist a backward glance at the camera after he had passed the photographer. Carts and waggons line the street and townspeople either walk casually down the centre of the road or stand around in small groups. The only motor visible is the elegant open-top car (EO 1**) parked outside the Wynnstay. The card was posted from Machynlleth in September 1912.

> Dear Flo, Arrived safe. It is very dull here I don't know what I shall do with myself . . .   (WHS Kingsway Real Photo Series.)

Heol Penrallt

The War Memorial, erected and unveiled on the Gruthun in 1924, now occupies the position of the photographer responsible for this view of Heol Penrallt, some fifteen years previously. Whilst there may be few physical differences between this and the present scene, mention must be made of the Tabernacle Arts Centre, established in the former Wesleyan Chapel, located between the buildings. This development has transformed the position of the arts in Machynlleth.

(Unused card, by J. Evans, Printer & Stationer, Machynlleth; Everton Series.)

An early post-war view of Heol Penrallt. The Town Hall which, in pre-Tabernacle days, was the main venue of concerts, dramas and eisteddfodau in the area, is prominent on the left. On the right, the railings survived the war-time scrap drive and still protect Aberllefenni House, for many years the main quarry office. The premises of the Machynlleth & District Co-operative Society next door are recessed, before two handsome shops which protrude slightly, owned by William and Frank Breese. Motor interest focuses mainly on three vehicles: from the left, an Austin 16—at this time very much 'the farmer's car'—whilst the Austin van facing it was the town's Fire Brigade, normally stored beneath the Town Hall. Finally, one of the vehicles near the clock was an early Standard Vanguard, with its distinctive stub tail, c.1952. *(A Real Photograph published by Photo Precision, St. Albans.)*

Royal House, the solicitor's and registrar's offices, the hair-dressers' that used to be Dick's Shoe Shop, G. M. Arthur's excellent food store, Tower Cafe, Peter Rees the butcher, Y Ford Gron and Harry Lewis's Bakery; all are faithfully recorded here as they were during the early 1960s. *(© Judges Postcards Ltd, Hastings 01424 420919.)*

A much earlier, reverse view of Heol Penrallt; the absence of the War Memorial is the most notable feature. The original photograph would date from around 1910, whilst the card was used postally in 1918:

> *We arrived here quite safely, but do you know we are on or at least half way up a mountain! but the view is glorious—will tell you all about it. This view is of the town 2 miles away. We are very isolated here but we just love wandering through the mountains. On Monday we are going to Aberistwith (sic).*
>
> (Park, Newtown, Mid Wales.)

Heol Pentrerhedyn

Up to the time of the First World War, the Lion Hotel had its own dedicated bus service to transport guests to and from the railway station; the bus is in the process of turning in to the hotel in this photograph taken c.1910-12. The card was posted in September 1916.

(WH Smith, Kingsway Real Photo Series.)

Plas, Machynlleth Fox Hounds, are normally considered a Foot Pack but on this occasion, at least ten members were mounted. Photographed 1912.

(Unused card; no imprint.)

Pentrerhedyn Street c. 1925. The bus waiting near the clock was to operate one of the services to Aberdyfi and Tywyn, introduced by the Corris Railway Company in 1924. The card, posted to Broad Green, Liverpool on 24 October, 1933 reads:

I'll bet you can't pronounce the name of this place where I'm staying to-night. Reached here at 6.00 p.m. after a wonderful day in Barmouth and round about Cader Idris. Aberystwyth to-morrow and then I start coming home. (Jones, Maglona Series.)

A pair of recently polled lime trees in Heol Pentrerhedyn frame this view of the clock dating from the mid 1950s. The card, posted to Llandovery (*sic*) in July 1959, carries the message:

Nid oeddwn yn gwybod tan nos Wener eich bod i ffwrdd . . .
[I did not know until Friday evening that you were away . . .]

(*Printed and Published by Harvey Barton & Son, Ltd, Bristol.*)

Heol Powys

Heol Powys shortly after construction, but before the end-of-terrace plots were occupied. The end property on the right was a sweet shop run by Mr and Mrs Jenkin Evans; the proximity of the Board School at the end of the road must have influenced the location of the business! John Evans, the printer, stands outside the wall by the shop, *à la* Hitchcock.

(*Unused card Published by J. Evans, Printer & Stationer, Machynlleth; Everton Series.*)

Lion Hotel

The Lion features, in part, in many cards of Heol Pentrerhedyn, but this is the only card yet encountered which concentrates on the hotel itself. The location of the name above the entrance to the car-park suggests a pre-war date, c.1938.

(Published by the Lion Hotel.)

Owain Glyndŵr's Parliament House

Nowadays, we can gain only the broadest impressions of the original building where Owain Glyndŵr assembled his historic parliament in 1404. Five hundred years, during which time countless changes were inflicted on the structure, were to pass before any real interest was taken in the remains of the building.

By the turn of the twentieth century the remnants served as rather shabby dwellings and when David Davies of Llandinam, in 1910, offered to restore them and also create an adjacent Institute for the benefit of the youth of the town, the offer was gladly accepted. The restoration of the Old Parliament House and the new Institute, located directly opposite the main entrance into the Plas, proved a timely improvement before the royal visit of 1911.

The few photographs taken before restoration can do little to represent the building of Owain's time other than rouse the imagination.

The remains of the old parliament building, within the context of Heol Maengwyn, looking east, c.1900. Card posted to Aberystwyth in July 1906:

> *Having a fine time of it . . .*   *(Valentine's Series.)*

This photographic card provides a better record of the structure, c.1900-10 and, incidentally, also demonstrates how cards could be used many years after their first appearance; this was posted to West Hamilton, Ontario, in April, 1928:

> *Dear Family, I am writing this for Mammie, who wants me to tell you she will send you an Epistle this coming week, so look out. Machynlleth and all that's in it, is very quiet, everything as per usual. Nothing of note.*

As the message lacks urgency and the postage was underpaid, it would hardly seem to have been worth the effort, yet the card is a survivor; it has been to Ontario, and returned to Wales.   *(Photochrom Real Photo, Tunbridge Wells.)*

The restored Parliament House, on the right, with the Institute and tower, on the left. The idea of a bowling green in this location, however, was not successful.

(Unused card; The Maglona Series, Valentine copyright.)

Plas

This fine print, addressed to James Dubet Esq., 'Au Passage', Laroche-Chalais, Dordogne, was clearly franked at Machynlleth at 9.45 a.m. on 27 July, 1907 and arrived at Laroche-Chalais the following day.

> *This was the country seat of the late Marchioness of Londonderry. Now her son Lord Herbert Vane-Tempest has it. He came down with our train . . .*

The card was obviously appreciated for it has been well preserved and, somehow, found its way back to Wales.

Interestingly, the original negative was amongst those sold by D. S. George to Valentine's of Dundee, and prints from it were marketed by them up to at least the 1960s.

(D. S. George & Son.)

The east elevation of the Plas features on this card published after the royal visit of 1911; it shows the house at its best and at the height of its importance.

(Maglona Series, by E. Alfred Jones, Londonderry House.)

The main drive of the Plas, photographed from within the grounds, looking north towards the wooden gates which gave access to Heol Maengwyn. The absence of a building where the Owain Glyndŵr Institute now stands, suggests that either the old structure on this site was painted out of the negative, or the photograph was taken after it had been demolished and before construction of the Institute had commenced, c.1910.

(Maglona Series, E. Alfred Jones, Londonderry House.)

The later Plas gates hang on the original pillars, c.1930.

(Maglona Series, E. Alfred Jones, Londonderry House.)

Post Office

Post Office staff posed proudly outside their new premises in 1910; the Telegram boy without a bike appears to have been equipped with a 'magic' carpet. The card was posted from Machynlleth on 24 July, 1910, to Mr C. H. Poston, in Liverpool, and the original message provides a fine caption:

> *I wonder do you know anybody in this group? It is the photograph of Machynlleth Post Office Staff, of which I shall be a member for some time. The office is a new one, it was only opened at the beginning of the year. Hope you are all well as we are here. Tom.*

How regrettable that we have no names for any of the group; which was Tom, one wonders?   *(Photographic card; no imprint.)*

Railway Station

The Dyfi valley floods have been countless over the years, causing farmers to move their stock to safety at short notice and, in the old days before early warning systems were introduced, often through the rising waters. Since the construction of the railway embankment in the early 1860s, most floods have been contained to the north of the railway but this flood c.1904, would appear to have been particularly severe. Unused photogravure card.   *(Maglona Series, E. Alfred Jones, Londonderry House.)*

Possibly taken from the same viewpoint, and on the same day as the previous view, but looking north, showing the Cambrian station in the foreground with horse buses from the hotels. Although only a photogravure card, it is possible to read the name of the Lion Hotel on the bus with a white roof. The Corris Railway's original station, with large lettering on the roof proclaiming 'for Cader Idris and Talyllyn Lake' may be seen beyond. c.1904.

(Maglona Series, E. Alfred Jones, Londonderry House.)

Several fine views exist of Machynlleth station. In this example, some railway staff were persuaded to pose alongside but none are recognisable save, possibly, the single figure near the poster hoarding, who appears to be W. E. Evans, the manager of the station bookstall – he was adept at appearing in many photographs at the station during the period before the First World War. The two figures on the left are enginemen, complete with their metal food boxes, on their way either to or from work, c.1907.

(J. Evans, Printer & Stationer, Machynlleth; Everton Series.)

This photogravure view completes the flood panorama but would seem to be based on a later photograph than the initial pair. Although indistinct, the Corris Railway bridge in the distance appears to be the later, girder version, constructed in 1906 and the large reserve of coal in the foreground suggests this view may date from the early period of the war, c.1916.   *(Exclusive Sepiatone series, published by the Photochrom Co. Ltd.)*

A LIVELY LOAD.
Arrived safely at MACHYNLLETH

Despite the caption, this was most certainly not taken on Machynlleth station, but was merely a general design over-printed to sell in the area. Nonetheless, it appears to have inspired the sender who posted it at Machynlleth in 1911 with the message:

I have seen Miss Evans safe off this morning. Took her to the station on our little truck. Meet her at stat. (sic) & take care of her. Drop a line before you come over, so that I can come to stat. with little truck . . . Harry.

Royal House

Fact and legend regarding Royal House have become intertwined over the years. We may accept that Dafydd Gam was imprisoned here (he died at Agincourt) and that Charles I possibly slept here *en route* to Chester, but any underground passage must surely have been much shorter than suggested, if it existed at all.

(Maglona Series, E. Alfred Jones, Londonderry House, c.1910.)

ROYAL HOUSE, MACHYNLLETH.

Here David Gam was imprisoned for eight years, 1404-12, for attempting to assassinate Owain Glyndwr when he was crowned King of Wales.

Here Charles I. slept on his way to Chester.

The bed in which he slept is in the possession of Col. Ruck at Esgair Hall.

An underground passage connects this house and Cefncaer Pennal (4 miles) on which at one time stood a large fort.

[Copyright.]

Royalty

A fine composite souvenir of the royal visit of 1911. The card was posted from Nottingham to Colour Sergeant Warburton of the Notts & Derbyshire Regiment, c/o the Stores Tent, Camp, Scarborough, on 4 August, 1911.

> *Dear father, Glad to hear you are alright . . .*

>   *(Maglona Series; E. Alfred Jones, Londonderry House.)*

Wynnstay

Superficially, a charming card, but with a message which would most certainly not be committed to an open postcard today. It was posted at Machynlleth, to the Rectory at Penegoes, on 21 November, 1907.

> *We have a fox to let out on the Park Common, tomorrow, Thursday, at 11 o'clock.*
> *Signed.*   *(Maglona Series; E. Alfred Jones, Londonderry House.)*

By the 1920s, the full name of the Wynnstay Herbert Arms & Unicorn Hotel had been shortened to the present Wynnstay Arms Hotel. The three motor-cars contribute to the distinctive atmosphere of the period.   *(Unused card, produced in the Trust House Series.)*

The appearance of the hotel changed little during the ensuing forty years although the shops in the area changed character and the Post Office vacated their premises during the 1990s, after over eighty years. Even by 2001, the Wynnstay is externally much the same despite many improvements made to its interior.

(Published by Photochrom Co. Ltd., for Trust House Ltd., c.1965.)

MALLWYD

Mallwyd is situated near the junction of the north-south A470 and the old coaching road to Welshpool, presently the A458, and at the heart of an area notorious for the activities during the sixteenth century of Gwylliaid Cochion Mawddwy (The red-haired bandits of Mawddwy). These are said to have terrorised the district and when eighty of their number were seized and 'punished according to their desserts' the survivors sought revenge by laying an ambush at a spot some two miles from Mallwyd, along the Welshpool road, still referred to as 'Llidiart y Barwn', where Baron Lewis Owen—one of those responsible for the capture of the majority of the gang—was assassinated.

A tinted photogravure card, of the view south towards Cwmllinau and Cemaes. Although not clearly portrayed, the church nestles amidst some very fine yew trees, near the distant bend in the road.

(Unused card, published by E. Evans, Post Office, Dinas Mawddwy, c.1920.)

A later view, from much the same location, but looking east. Before being named The Brigand's Inn, to re-inforce the association with the Gwylliaid Cochion, the inn was known as Bury's Hotel. The Vauxhall Velox and the attractive classic car alongside suggest a date c.1963-5 for the original photograph.   *(Unused card; no imprint.)*

Comparatively recent road improvements on the A470 in the vicinity of the Brigand's Inn have seen the upper of these two bridges demolished to take the new, wider carriageway; the older pack-horse bridge, however, survives intact beneath the new bridge.

(Unused card by J. Jones, Grocer, Mallwyd, c. 1920, courtesy of Mrs G. Burton.)

PANTPERTHOG

Pantperthog, seen from the old Corris road, c.1900. Llwyngwern station would have been to the right of this composition. The card was posted in 1924.

(Park Series, Newtown.)

A river scene from the Pantparthog/Llwyngwern area.

(Unused card, D. S. George & Son, courtesy of The National Library of Wales, Aberystwyth.)

PENEGOES

Situated just 2 miles from the centre of Machynlleth, Penegoes is notable as the birthplace of Richard Wilson, respected Royal Academican, precursor of Constable and Turner, and the man most often referred to as the father of British landscape painting. Although it appears that his association with Penegoes was but brief, it is regrettable that he receives so little general recognition in the area. No work representing Wilson is exhibited locally, although the *Montgomeryshire Express* of 5 July, 1947, carried a report that Richard Wilson 'etchings' had been presented to Machynlleth Urban District Council who, previously, had 'only one small painting' by this artist. Where are those etchings and the one small painting now, one wonders?

The rectory at Penegoes, where Wilson was born in 1714. This photogravure card was used postally on 22 August, 1919.

(Printed & Published by Evan Jones, Machynlleth; Maglona Series No. 2.)

Tai newyddion, c.1920; unused card.

(Published by Evans and Sons, Grocers etc., Penegoes, Mont.)

The village post office, c.1920. Not used postally but annotated on the reverse:

Pob hapusrwydd yn y cartref cysurus. [Every happiness in the comfortable home].

(Published by Evans and Sons, Grocers etc., Pengoes, Mont.)

PENNAL

Pennal is steeped in Welsh history, from the time the Romans built a fort at nearby Cefn Caer to the Owain Glyndŵr period when the Welsh prince sent a letter to the King of France, in 1402, seeking an alliance to free the Church from the influence of Canterbury.

Interest in Owain's letter was renewed at the approach of the new millennium, when representations were made for the letter's return to Wales. The *Archives Nationales*, in Paris, the present custodians, allowed it to return on loan to Wales and from April 2000 it was exhibited for nearly six months at the National Library at Aberystwyth.

A fine view of Pennal, looking west towards Cwrt, in the right-hand distance, where the road bifurcates; the right-hand route may be glimpsed climbing toward Pen-y-bwlch and Cwm Maethlon. The complete absence of road traffic and what appears to be an unmodernised facade of the Lion Hotel which may just be glimpsed beyond the church, suggest a date c.1925; judging by the amount of washing drying on clothes-lines and hedgerows, it may well have been a Monday!

(D. S. George & Son.)

Although the river is visible, Llyn-y-bwtri lies just east (to the left) of this later view of Pennal. The card was used postally on 7 November, 1939 but, interestingly, the original photograph, which would have dated from around 1936-7 appears not to be as 'sharp' as would normally be expected from D. S. George & Son.

Yet another fine example of Donald Stuart George's photographic coverage of the area – Cwmffernol is on the minor road from Cwrt to Tywyn. For many years, the house was occupied by Catherine Pugh and her brother – could she be the figure silhouetted in the doorway? The card was posted in Machynlleth on 4 September, 1906, with a simple message, in a juvenile hand: *Love from Leonard.* (D. S. George & Son, c, 1905.)

STAYLITTLE AND DYLIFE

The area around Staylittle, due east, and Dylife, just a mile or so west of the location portrayed here, was ravaged in the pursuit of minerals, notably lead, during the nineteenth century. Initially, the ore was carted down the steep gradients to Derwenlas for transfer to the river boats; later, it was taken down more gentle grades to the railway at Llanbrynmair.

The scattered community at Dylife, during the 1880s, was able to boast a row of cottages, a Plas near Esgairgaled, and further cottages near the Star Inn. There were then also two chapels, St David's Church and Vicarage as well as a small school and post office. Staylittle was more rural.

At Dylife, today, only the Star Inn keeps company with the surviving farms and row of Forestry Workers' cottages. Most traces of mining have disappeared; only the remains of spoil heaps serve to remind us of the area's industrial past.

MNLH.75 The Pennant Valley, Staylittle, Dylife Road, MACHYNLLETH Copyright Frith's

Thankfully, this region avoided despoilation, and the glorious view, looking north down Cwm Pennant, remains unimpaired. The card was used postally, by 'Auntie Rose' from Llandrindod Wells to Acton, in September, 1956:

> We had a breakdown 11 miles from here . . . they had to phone for another coach but hope to have ours ready by the a.m., else the driver will have to phone Brighton for another coach which will have to travel up all night.

(Courtesy The Francis Frith Collection, www.francisfrith.co.uk)

TAL-Y-LLYN

The attractions of Tal-y-llyn lake and the two hospitable hostelries set against the majestic lower slopes of Cader Idris, proved magnetic as far as Victorian and Edwardian tourists were concerned. At that time, few visitors to the coastal resorts ventured to return home without sampling the delights of an excursion inland; both the Llyfnant Valley and Tal-y-llyn were popular destinations. In the case of the latter, the Cambrian and Corris Railways played their part in getting 'visitors' within striking distance of their goal, usually as far as Corris; thereafter, horse-drawn waggonettes and, later, motor charabancs were used to reach the final destination.

Some tourists came via the Tal-y-llyn Railway but the Corris Railway was particularly successful at attracting summer visitors. During the late 1880s, for example, fully 160,000 passenger per annum experienced the delights of a journey on the narrow-gauge to Corris *en route* to welcoming hotels at the western extremity of Tal-y-llyn lake.

The archetypal view of Tal-y-llyn, showing the well-stocked and tended vegetable garden alongside Ty'n-y-cornel Hotel. The card was posted at Corris in May, 1904 with the plea:
When are you going to send me some P.C. (sic)

(*The Wrench Series; Printed in Saxony.*)

This view of the neighbouring Pen-y-bont Hotel is typical of many photographs that were taken from the elevated ground alongside the ancient church which, according to J. Arthur Williams in *Trem yn Ôl* (Gwynedd Archives, 1963) dates from the ninth century. This was a popular terminus for vehicles from Tywyn/Abergynolwyn, as well as Corris. The card carries no imprint other than 'Printed in Germany'; it was used postally from Towyn (sic) in September 1906.

Another photogravure card looking west and featuring a stretch of road which, over the years, has proved troublesome and expensive to maintain. This card is another from the transitionary period which, although providing a small area for a message on the reverse, continued to leave a space beneath the illustration, in the old style. Some cards in the Wrench Series carry an additional imprint in red—*Gwladgarwr*; it would be good to know more of this particular 'patriot'.   *(Unused Wrench Series Card; Printed in Berlin, c.1905.)*

Sometimes referred to as Dolau Cae. There was a house on this site in the fourteenth century but perhaps the most famous resident in more recent times was Mr Howell Idris, MP, originally a native of Corris who emigrated to London where he established the 'Idris Table Waters Company'. The path visible on the left is one of the recognised routes to Llyn Cau and the summit of Cader Idris. This photographic card was used postally from Machynlleth in August 1908, but carries no imprint, save an interesting restriction above the message area, on the reverse: *This space may be used for communication to all countries except United States, Spain and Japan.*

Narrow, twisting roads in Wales often attract adverse criticism and it is easy to disregard the improvements which have been made over the years, until we chance upon a view like this which reminds us of the narrow carriageways of pioneer motoring days. The open car and motor-cycle combination suggest a date around 1920; the card was posted at Corris in 1928.

We have just had dinner at this little place . . . if we come to Borth another year it would be fine to stay here for 2 or 3 days to fish in the lake . . . Doris is not going to Barbers as there is no maid & it would be too much . . .

(Lilywhite Ltd., Guaranteed Real Photo and British Manufacture.)

The road along the pass was blocked by a landslide on 18 July, 1926. Whether the open-topped GWR bus from Dolgellau brought tourists to view the damage, or whether it had intended making its way down to the lake, is not apparent.   *(D. S. George & Son.)*

The following year, the road was severed again, this time by a chasm which appeared near the site of the previous disaster. 24 June, 1927.   *(D. S. George & Son.)*

Capel Ystradgwyn, the small building on the left, situated alongside the B4405 between Minffordd and the lake, near the photographer's position for the photograph of Dolau Cau (p. 105). It was erected c.1829 and re-built 1896. In addition to religious services, the little chapel was used for other social events, when the restricted space would be packed to capacity for concerts and eisteddfodau. This card was used postally in 1949.

(D. S. George & Son.)

Mynydd Rugog forms an attractive backdrop to the Ty'n-y-cornel Hotel and lake at Tal-y-llyn. The Welsh name, Llyn Mwyngil (lake of the pleasant retreat) is rarely used today, but the mile-long stretch of fresh water is well stocked with fine trout and continues to attract those who fish for sport. Photograph c.1939.

(D. S. George & Son.)

This view of Pen-y-bont Hotel, Tal-y-llyn Lake, was posted at Corris on 13 July, 1912 and carries the observation that 'the landlord and our driver are talking away in Welsh outside the window.'   *(Photographic card by D. S. George & Son.)*

A view of the road along the pass as it was mid-century; although it appears in fine condition at the time of this photograph, it required further, and expensive, attention as recently as 1994 when three large cavities beneath the surface had to be repaired.
(A Real Photograph, published in the 'Maglona' Series by Jones, Corner Shop, Machynlleth, c.1950.)

Acknowledgement

My grateful thanks are extended to Dr D. Huw Owen, formerly Keeper of the Pictures and Maps at the National Library of Wales, Aberystwyth, for preparing the Foreword. I am also indebted to the National Library for allowing the use of some of its own material; the Library staff, particularly William Troughton and Rhodri Morgan on this occasion, were most helpful. Others who repaired some of the deficiencies within my own collection were the Corris Railway Society and Mrs G. Burton, of Cwmllinau. Medwyn Parry, of the Royal Commission on the Ancient and Historical Monuments of Wales, also assisted with valuable information, as did Dafydd Wyn James, Mallwyd, Hefin Williams, Cwmllinau, W. H. S. Davies, Tywyn and Maureen and Alfred Hughes, Machynlleth.

Most of the picture postcard publishers represented herein have not survived into the twenty-first century, but a handful of the more famous names remain. The Francis Frith Collection, Salisbury, Wiltshire SP3 5QP, www.francisfrith.co.uk have kindly sanctioned the use of four cards from their famous collection, whilst Judges Postcards Ltd., Hastings (01424 420919) allowed six of their excellent cards to be reproduced; W. H. Smith of Swindon, kindly approved free use of four cards from the Kingsway Series. None, however, have been more generous than the Library of St. Andrew's University, Fife, custodians of the historic collection of Valentine's of Dundee. No fewer than 25 examples from the Valentine Collection have been included. This vast and valuable archive even manages to increase marginally, from time to time, as occasional cards are discovered which are 'new' to the Library (01334 462 339).

Throughout the volume, all publishers are credited individually beneath each image, as appropriate, but if any surviving company has been overlooked by the author, the omission is unintentional. Please advise Gomer Press of any oversight.

Gwyn Briwnant Jones
Cardiff, 2002.

Bibliography

BICK, David *Dylife*, 1985, The Pound House, Newport.

BRIWNANT JONES, Gwyn *Railway Through Talerddig*, 1990, Gomer Press.

COZENS, Lewis *The Corris Railway*, 1949, Corris Railway Society.

DAVIES, David Wyn *Machynlleth Town Trail*, 1981, Machynlleth Civic Society.

DAVIES, David Wyn *The Town of a Prince*, 1991, Machynlleth Rotary.

DAVIES, David Wyn *Pictorial History of Machynlleth*, 1996, Machynlleth Civic Society.

LLOYD, Thomas *The Lost Houses of Wales*, 1986, SAVE.

PAGE, Hugh E. *Rambles around the Cambrian Coast*, 1936, GWR.

ROBERTS, Askew *Gossiping Guide to Wales*, 1900, Woodall, Minshall & Thomas.

TURNER, Godfrey *Picturesque Wales*, 1890, Cambrian Railways.

WILLIAMS, J. Arthur *Trem yn Ôl*, 1963, Archifdy Meirion.

Also, a copy of *The Machynlleth Town Guide*, 1949, and an article by Sara Eade on D. S. George & Son in *Picture Postcard Monthly*, October, 1994.

Back cover illustration: Machynlleth
This early card (c. 1902) was discovered in April 2002. Judging by various elements within the composition – lack of pavements and low wall around the Wynnstay Hotel; a town house where the Barclays Bank now stands, and what appear to be a pair of light globes at the base of the clock tower – this view could date from around 1885-1890. It was used as a Christmas Card by Kate Evans, Maengwyn Steet, Machynlleth. [No imprint].